PRIMARY EXPLORERS

ANIMALS

igloo

Contents

BACKBONES

Animals with backbones are called vertebrates. Limbs, such as legs, are attached to the backbone, which also supports the head. Mammals, birds, reptiles, amphibians and fish are all vertebrates.

AMAZING ANIMALS

Planet Earth is home to a huge range of living things that breathe, feed and grow.

Animals are living things that also move. Many of them have muscles that are used to walk, swim, slither, fly or crawl. Animals have senses, such as sight, taste and touch, which give them useful information about the world around them.

Great senses of sight, smell and hearing help the mighty leopard to find and track down its prey. Its body combines speed, strength and superb climbing skills.

Animals that do not have backbones are called invertebrates. This is a huge group of animals that includes insects, spiders, scorpions, crabs, shelled animals and worms. While most invertebrates are smaller than vertebrates, there are plenty of exceptions, such as giant octopuses. About 95 per cent of all animals alive on Earth are invertebrates.

DID YOU KNOW?

Giant tortoises have the longest lives of any land animals. They can live for more than 150 years.

LIFE CYCLES

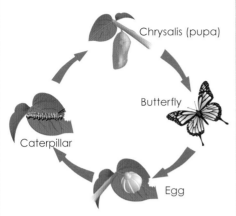

Chrysalis (pupa)

Butterfly

Caterpillar

Egg

Animals reproduce: this means that they have young. The way that an animal grows, changes, has young and later dies is called a life cycle. A butterfly has a four-stage life cycle – egg, caterpillar, chrysalis (or pupa), then butterfly.

Reptile

Fish

Insect

Amphibian

Arachnid

Mammal

Bird

Animals are divided into groups, according to their body shapes, how their bodies work and the way that the animals behave.

ALL SHAPES AND SIZES

Animals are made of cells, which are the building blocks of living things. Some animals are so tiny they have just one cell and can only be seen with a microscope. Others, such as the blue whale, are enormous. Their cells are organized into organs, such as stomachs, brains and lungs, and limbs. Legs, arms and wings are all types of limb.

Single-celled animals are called protists. They were discovered over 300 years ago, after microscopes had been invented.

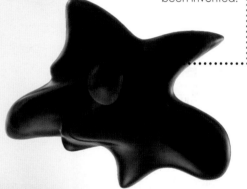

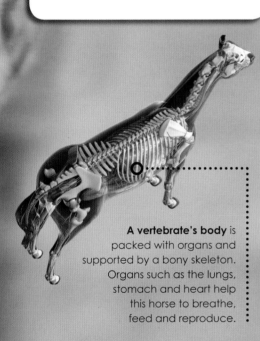

A vertebrate's body is packed with organs and supported by a bony skeleton. Organs such as the lungs, stomach and heart help this horse to breathe, feed and reproduce.

DID YOU KNOW?

Scientists have identified more than two million different types, or species, of animals so far, and there are plenty more still waiting to be discovered.

LIFESTYLES

Animals behave in a huge variety of ways. They hunt for food, rest, find mates, look after their young, communicate with one another and make shelters. These paper wasps have made an elaborate waterproof nest to protect their eggs.

HABITATS

Tropical rainforests grow near the Equator, where the climate is always warm and wet. Plants grow well in these conditions, and provide food for many species, or types, of animals.

Deserts are places where less than 15 cm (6 in) of rain falls in a whole year. This habitat supports little plant life, and animals struggle to survive here.

Ponds are freshwater habitats. They are delicate environments that are easily damaged by pollution.

WHERE ANIMALS LIVE

The place that an animal lives is called its habitat.

A habitat is not just a place. It includes the other animals or plants that live in an area, and it is affected by the landscape, the seasons and the climate, or weather. Habitats on land, such as grasslands and forests, are described as terrestrial. The oceans are the largest habitat of all.

DID YOU KNOW?

Animals are suited to life in particular habitats. If those habitats are destroyed, some animal species are likely to die out forever.

The stunning white fur of an Arctic fox helps this mammal to survive the winter in its snowy habitat. Its thick coat is one of the warmest of any animal, and being white helps it to hide from its prey.

LIFE ON LAND

Animals that live on land have to cope with the weather. Deserts are very dry places, and creatures that live there have to survive for a long time without water. Many deserts can be extremely hot in the day, but bitterly cold at night. Animals that live in cold places, such as polar bears and penguins, have to deal with freezing temperatures.

CITY LIFE

Many animals, such as foxes, raccoons and sometimes even bears, thrive in urban habitats – in cities and towns. They can scavenge food from the rubbish left behind by humans, and find shelter from the weather.

LIFE IN WATER

More than 70 per cent of our planet Earth is covered in water. Watery habitats, such as rivers and seas, are described as aquatic environments. More animals live in water than on land, and their bodies are suited for movement underwater.

Coral reefs are unusual ocean habitats that can support millions of living creatures. Reefs are formed by tiny living animals, called polyps, that build rocky cups to sit in.

MAMMAL FEATURES

Most mammals give birth to live young, rather than laying eggs. The babies, like this little macaque, are often helpless at first.

Mammal mothers feed their young with milk and look after them while they grow. These piglets are drinking their mother's milk.

Mammals are able to live in hot and cold places, because they are able to control their body temperatures. Long, thick fur, like this snow leopard's, can help to keep them warm.

MAMMALS

A mammal is an animal with fur, or hair. It feeds its young with milk.

There are about 5,000 different species of mammal, including us humans. Most mammals live on land, but some types have evolved (changed over time) to live in water. Most mammal bodies are covered with hair, which helps them to stay warm.

DID YOU KNOW?
A baby echidna is called a puggle! It is born blind and bald, but grows spines over the next four weeks.

MONOTREMES

Monotremes are the only mammals to lay eggs. They all live in Australia, Tasmania and New Guinea. There are only five species of monotremes, including duck-billed platypuses and echidnas. Echidnas have slender, beak-like mouths and rounded bodies covered in spines.

Echidnas have both spines and fur, which is an unusual combination for any animal. These monotremes eat ants, worms and grubs.

MARSUPIALS

Marsupials are mammals that give birth to tiny young that continue to grow inside their mother's pouch. Kangaroos, wallabies, opossums, quolls, Tasmanian devils and koalas are all types of marsupial. The world's largest marsupial is the red kangaroo, which lives in the deserts and grasslands of Australia.

DUCK-BILLED PLATYPUS

The strange-looking duck-billed platypus is a monotreme. It lives in rivers and lakes, and uses its sensitive bill to search the mud for small animals to eat. Platypuses are mostly nocturnal, which means they are active at night and rest in the daytime.

Red kangaroos can bound along at speeds of 30 mph (48 km/h). These marsupials have a superb sense of smell that they use to find water, which is scarce in their normal habitat.

A baby kangaroo is called a joey. It stays in its mother's pouch for about 190 days before emerging for the first time.

CATS AND DOGS

Cats and dogs are predators. They hunt other animals to eat.

Predators need to be able to find, catch and eat their prey. Being a hunter takes special skills, as well as a body equipped with excellent senses and fast reactions. They have strong jaws, sharp teeth, powerful muscles and, in the cat family, powerful claws.

A grey wolf stalks its prey through a marsh. It hunts for animals as large as deer.

WOLVES

Wolves are the largest members of the dog family – the canids. Canids have deep, strong bodies and are able to pursue their prey over long distances before tiring. Their teeth are long and sharp, but their claws are blunt and short. Grey wolves are the ancestors of all modern pet dogs, but they are wild, aggressive animals. They live in the forests of northern Europe and Asia.

WORKING TOGETHER

Most predators hunt alone, but those that hunt in packs are able to chase bigger prey by working together. Lions, wolves, coyotes and African hunting dogs all live and hunt in groups. The hunters share their catch with the rest of the group.

CARNIVORE TEETH

Cats, such as tigers, and dogs are carnivores. They use their teeth to grab hold of struggling victims, to pierce and slice flesh, and to crunch bones.

A pack of African hunting dogs has strength in numbers when it attacks a hyena in the hope of stealing its catch. The hyena must give up or risk injury, or even death.

CARNIVORES

Carnivores, such as cats and dogs, eat only meat. Cats have superb senses of smell and sight, so they can detect their prey from far away. Unlike dogs, most species of cats live and hunt alone. There are about 38 species of cat.

A spotted coat may help leopards to hide in the dappled light of their forest homes.

The sharp, curved claws of a cat help the animal to climb trees, and are perfect for grabbing hold of prey.

DID YOU KNOW?

The smallest canid is the fennec fox, which lives in the deserts of Africa. Its body length is about 30 cm (12 in), but its huge ears grow up to 15 cm (6 in) long.

Leopards are powerful predators and great survivors. They are very adaptable animals and live in a range of habitats.

BEARS

Bears are large mammals with powerful but short legs, large heads and a great sense of smell.

Most bears live in forests, where they hunt other animals for food – including fish – or they eat berries, fruit, plant shoots and insects. They have few natural enemies, except humans. There are eight species of bear, including polar bears, sloth bears and giant pandas.

BEAR CUBS

Bear cubs are often born during the winter months, when their mothers are resting in dens. During the winter it is hard to find food, so resting is a good way to survive. The mothers have stores of body fat, which their bodies use to make milk for the cubs. Here, a polar bear and her cub rest on the ice in the frozen Arctic.

GIANT PANDAS

Unlike other bears, giant pandas rarely eat any type of meat. Most of their diet is bamboo, and they live in bamboo forests in a mountainous region of southwest China. Pandas have a long bone in each wrist that works like an extra finger. It enables them to grab hold of bamboo stems and leaves.

Giant pandas face extinction in the wild because more than half of their bamboo forests have been destroyed since the 1970s. When panda cubs are newborn, they are pink, tiny and totally helpless. It is normal for two cubs to be born at a time, but only the strongest one survives.

DID YOU KNOW?
Of the eight species of bear, six are in danger of becoming extinct.

Each summer, Alaskan grizzly bears gather in groups to feast on salmon that are moving upstream to lay their eggs. When a male grizzly stands on its back feet it can measure 3 m (10 ft) tall. Grizzly bears can run faster than most humans.

GRIZZLIES
Grizzlies are a type of brown bear. They have long, thick fur and live in North America. Grizzlies have enormous teeth and huge claws that grow to 10 cm (4 in) in length. Enormous teeth, paws and claws are useful for grabbing salmon from the water.

UNLIKELY-LOOKING COUSINS

Seals, such as this young grey seal, sea lions and walruses belong to a group of animals called pinnipeds, and they are closely related to bears. These animals live in aquatic habitats. With streamlined bodies, flippers and short fur, they are well suited to swimming.

GRASSLAND GRAZERS

Grazing mammals eat a low-energy diet of grass and other plants.

Horses, deer, antelope and cattle are all grazing animals with hoofed feet – most of them live in grassland habitats. Animals that live on a diet of plant matter are called herbivores. They have strong teeth that they use to grind the stems of tough grasses.

Grazers can struggle to survive in cold winters. These deer must find food beneath thick snow, and look out for hungry predators.

ELEPHANTS

Elephants are grazing animals, and the largest of all creatures that live on land. They spend 16 to 18 hours a day feeding. Thanks to their trunks, which are muscular extensions of their upper lips and noses, elephants can reach up to trees to strip bark, shoots and tender leaves to eat. Unlike many other grazers, elephants don't have hooves. They have flat, fleshy feet that they can use to paw the ground and dig up roots to eat.

ALERT ANIMALS

Grazing animals spend most of their day eating, because grasses and leaves are poor in energy. Standing and eating on grasslands puts the grazers at risk from predators, so they have evolved special skills to keep themselves safe. Horses and deer, for example, are fast runners with excellent senses of hearing, smell and sight. Their eyes are on the sides of their heads, so they can see in several directions and spot advancing predators on the horizon.

DID YOU KNOW?

No one knows why zebras have black and white stripes, but it is thought that when herds of zebras gather together, the pattern confuses predators.

ON THE MOVE

Wildebeest, or gnus, are African antelopes that are related to cattle. They live in enormous herds and every year they make journeys, or migrations, that cover hundreds of miles. These migrations are necessary to find fresh grass growing in regions where seasonal rains have fallen.

During Africa's largest migration more than two million wildebeest cross the Masai Mara and Serengeti reserves. This incredible trek is necessary for the animals' survival.

RHINOS

Rhinos are large herbivores from Africa and Asia. All rhinos are endangered, which means they may become extinct in the near future. Their horns are used in traditional medicines, so poachers make money by killing rhinos and selling their horns. Poor eyesight makes the rhinos even more vulnerable.

Most grazing animals, such as these zebras in Africa, gather in herds because there is safety in numbers. All herd members look out for predators, and protect young animals.

MONKEYS AND APES

Chimps, gorillas, monkeys and humans belong to a group of animals called primates.

These intelligent animals usually live in family groups. Most monkeys and apes live in tropical rainforests, where they feed on fruits, leaves, insects and other small animals. Primates have large brains and flat nails on their fingers, rather than claws. Monkeys have tails, but apes do not.

GREAT APES

Chimps, bonobos, gibbons, gorillas and orangutans are called great apes, and they are our closest living relatives. Great apes not only look quite like us, but they often behave like humans, too. They teach their young, they are fast learners and they can use tools to get food. Some apes have even been taught how to "talk" with humans using sign language.

APE FEATURES

Like humans, chimps are able to show anger and happiness in their faces.

Orangutans use leaves to protect their heads from the rain, and to wipe their fur after eating messy food!

Smart Japanese macaques have learned how to keep warm in the winter. They bathe in the hot springs at their mountain home of Honshu, Japan.

DID YOU KNOW?

The smallest primates in the world are pygmy mouse lemurs. They weigh just 30 g (1 oz) and their bodies measure no more than 7.5 cm (3 in).

After watching humans, some orangutans learned how to row boats just by paddling with their hands.

SPIDER MONKEYS

Spider monkeys have long tails that they can use like a fifth limb. As they leap through trees, spider monkeys use their tails to balance and to grip tightly on to branches.

LEMURS

The island of Madagascar, off the eastern coast of Africa, is home to a group of primates called lemurs. They use all four limbs to leap and climb through trees, and can use their hands to grab hold of branches as they run and jump. Ring-tailed lemurs wave their stripy tails in the air to communicate with one another.

This ring-tailed lemur is still just a baby at six weeks old, but it can already climb trees. It will stay with its mother until it is one year old.

Chimps learn how to find food by watching older relatives. When a chimp pokes a stick into a termite mound, it comes out covered in tasty termites.

BATS

Some mammals are able to glide through the air, but bats are the only mammals that can fly.

A bat's wings are made from a double layer of skin that stretches from their body across the long, slender bones of their forelimbs. Bats are swift and agile in flight – they are able to change direction quickly and swoop through trees with ease. There are two types of bats: micro-bats and mega-bats.

VAMPIRE BATS

Vampire bats really do exist! These bats scrape flesh from their victims, such as birds or farm animals, and lap up the blood that oozes out. They do occasionally attack humans, but it is rare.

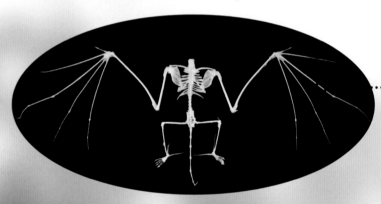

A bat skeleton (shown here without the skull) has the same basic bony structure as that of other vertebrates. The arm and finger bones, however, are extremely long, and are used to support the muscles and skin that stretch across a bat's wings.

It was once thought that micro-bats only used their echolocation skills to catch prey. In fact, they also use their calls to recognize each other and bats from nearby groups.

MICRO-BATS

Most bats are micro-bats, which are small and nocturnal. They are able to locate their prey, such as moths, by echolocation. The bats produce sounds, called clicks, which reflect off objects nearby, creating echoes. The bats hear these echoes, and use them to calculate the distance and size of their prey.

Some long-eared micro-bats have ears that are almost as long as their bodies. These enormous ears help them to echolocate.

MEGA-BATS
Mega-bats are active in the daytime. The largest mega-bat is the flying fox, with a wingspan of 1.5 m (5 ft). It feasts on trees that are laden with fruit. Flying foxes live in large groups called colonies.

This flying fox bat has large eyes and small ears because it relies on sight, not sound, to find food. Like all bats, it hangs upside-down when it rests.

The wingspan of a flying fox is ten times bigger than that of the smallest micro-bat, which has a wingspan of just 6 in (15 cm).

DID YOU KNOW?
Disk-winged bats from Central and South America have sticky disks on each wing. These enable them to walk up smooth surfaces, such as window panes!

SPOTTER'S GUIDE

WHALES AND DOLPHINS

Mammals that spend all of their lives in the oceans are called cetaceans.

Whales and dolphins need to swim to the surface to breathe air, but they feed, rest, mate and give birth underwater. They have unusual respiratory (breathing) and circulatory (blood) systems that allow them to dive into the deep oceans and stay there for 40 minutes or more before they need to come up for air.

Blue whales are the world's biggest animals. They can grow up to 30 m (98 ft) long. A type of baleen whale, they feed on small crustaceans called krill.

Sperm whales have teeth and prey on squid, octopus and fish. They are the world's largest carnivores, growing up to 20 m (65 ft) long.

Dolphins are small toothed cetaceans. They mostly hunt fish and often live in large family groups, called pods.

DID YOU KNOW?

River dolphins are almost blind and rely on the echolocation sound system to find their way around.

Giant humpback whales often leap out of the water and land with an enormous splash. The reason why humpbacks do this is still unknown.

STRONG SWIMMERS

Cetaceans no longer have legs or fur. Their large, fish-shaped bodies are packed with swimming muscles and their fore-limbs have evolved to become flippers, which they use to steer. The fin on a whale's back prevents it rolling over and powerful tail fins, called flukes, help to power the heavy body through the water.

Killer whales, or orcas, are easy to recognize with their distinctive black and white markings. These whales are highly intelligent and can hunt in packs. Orcas live in all the world's oceans.

Dolphins talk to each other using clicks, whistles and squeaks. They also use a type of echolocation (like bats) to find prey. They make sound in their noses by blowing air through folds of flesh that can be moved like lips.

DEEP SEA FEEDERS

Toothed whales and dolphins hunt prey such as fish and squid. Baleen whales, however, feast on tiny crustaceans. In their mouths they have two rows of horned plates, called baleens, that act like sieves. As they swim through shoals of crustaceans, they suck the water through the plates. The food animals get trapped, and are swallowed.

DID YOU KNOW?

Cetaceans have thick fat, called blubber, to help them stay warm. The blubber of a bowhead whale, which lives in icy Arctic waters, is 50 cm (20 in) thick!

OTTERS

Like cetaceans, otters are mammals that are suited to life underwater. They have long, narrow bodies and webbed feet. Most otters live in rivers, returning to land to rest in dens and burrows. They eat fish, crabs and frogs, and can stay underwater for some time while they hunt.

BIRDS

Birds are egg-laying vertebrates with feathers.

Birds belong to a hugely varied group of animals – there are about 9,000 species. The earliest-known bird lived about 150 million years ago, during the time of the dinosaurs, and probably evolved from a reptile. Most birds can fly, and this special skill has enabled them to travel to new habitats and evolve into many different shapes and sizes.

Male ostriches have black plumage (feathers), but females are brown. Both sexes have a thin coat of wispy feathers, called down, on the head and neck.

BIRD FEATURES

All birds lay eggs, in which the young develop and grow. Female birds would not be able to fly if they had to carry their young. Here, a black swan is settling down to incubate her eggs (keep them warm).

A bird's mouth is called a beak, or bill. Birds do not have teeth – they swallow their food whole.

Feathers are made from keratin, the same material that makes hair, nails and snake scales. Different types of feathers are needed for different things, such as flying or keeping warm.

DID YOU KNOW?

Swifts are small birds that spend almost all their lives in the air. They feed, mate and even sleep while soaring through the sky.

FLIGHTLESS BIRDS

Some birds are too big to fly. Ostriches are the world's largest birds – they can grow to 2.7 m (9 ft) tall. Most birds have four toes on each foot, but ostriches have just two. They can run at 45 mph (70 km/h) and kick out with their powerful legs if attacked. The world's rarest flightless birds are called kakapos. These parrots are active at night and walk long distances to chew plants. They only live on three small islands of New Zealand. Other flightless birds include emus, kiwis and cassowaries.

Many birds, including Canada geese, may migrate to warmer areas when winter is on the way.

FLOCKS

Some birds live together in a large group, called a flock. Red-billed queleas are seed-eating birds that live south of the Sahara desert. When they settle to feed, they can devour entire crops of corn and rice. Birds that flock are able to spend more time feeding, and less time watching out for predators.

Mute swans are one of the world's heaviest flying birds. Males and females stay together for life. They build their nests on the ground near the water's edge.

Thousands of queleas live in a single flock. They are thought to be the world's most common bird.

BIRD BONES

Birds need light, but strong, bodies in order to fly. Their bones are particularly small, but many of them are joined together to make a strong, rigid frame. Most birds also have hollow bones.

WATER BIRDS

Many types of birds live in, or near, water.

The oceans and rivers are full of animals that birds like to eat, especially fish. Webbed feet help water birds to move through water. Their feathers are coated with oils that stop them from becoming water-logged, and their bills are often long and slender – perfect for catching fish or digging small animals out of mud and sand.

DID YOU KNOW?
Emperor penguins can stay under water for up to 18 minutes at a time.

Up to a million lesser flamingos feed in Africa's Lake Nakuru, creating a sea of pink, feathery bodies.

There are five species of flamingo and they live in warm, watery regions. Flamingos survive by feeding in water that is too salty for most other birds.

Of all water birds, penguins are the most extraordinary. These flightless birds have bodies that are superbly suited to a life in water. Their wings work like flippers, and a thick layer of fat and waterproof feathers keep them warm and dry.

PENGUINS

While all water birds have to come to land to build nests, mate and lay eggs, some of them spend most of their time in water. Penguins have bodies that are so well adapted for swimming and hunting fish in the sea, that they have lost the ability to fly. Penguins live in the southern half of the world, and some species – such as king and emperor penguins – can survive the freezing winters of the Antarctic.

FLAMINGOS

African flamingos eat a diet of small water animals, especially crustaceans. They feed by hanging their heads upside-down, so their bills are underwater. Flamingos' food contains a pinkish pigment that is stored in their feathers. Adult birds can range from light pink to bright red.

American avocets have long, slender bills. They feed by swishing their bills from side to side underwater.

KINGFISHERS

Kingfishers live near freshwater, especially free-flowing rivers. They have superb eyesight that allows them to see, chase and grab fish, even when they are underwater.

DID YOU KNOW?

Snow geese travel up to 3,100 miles (5,000 km) when they fly south from their breeding grounds in the Arctic, to spend winter in warmer places. In spring they fly back again.

SINGERS, HUNTERS AND SHOW-OFFS

The smallest birds suck nectar from flowers, while some of the biggest are hunters.

Most birds belong to a group called the passerines and live in trees. They are also known as perching birds, because they can grip onto thin branches using their four-toed feet. Three toes point forwards and one is turned backwards. Birds of prey (raptors), however, have specially-adapted feet called talons. Each talon has four razor-sharp claws, used to catch other animals.

SINGING BIRDS

Passerines, such as thrushes, swallows, wagtails and warblers, live in many habitats, from forests to gardens. Most types of passerine bird have their own song. Some birds are born knowing their song, while others learn it from their parents. Passerines use their songs to mark out their living areas, or territories, and to get the attention of possible mates.

A male common yellowthroat sings a song that sounds like "wich-i-ty, wich-i-ty" to keep other birds out of his territory.

DID YOU KNOW?

Hyacinth macaws have long, tough bills that are strong enough to crush large palm nuts. These parrots live in S outh American rainforests.

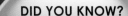

DID YOU KNOW?
Tiny hummingbirds can flap their wings up to 90 times a second as they suck sweet nectar from flowers.

With a wingspan of 2.1 m (7 ft), a golden eagle is an awesome predator. It can see prey from far away, and swoop in for the kill.

RAPTORS

Raptors are large carnivores that hunt other animals, and sometimes other birds, to eat. They have excellent eyesight and some can even detect the tiniest movement of a mouse scuttling through grass.

BIRDS ON PARADE

Many male birds have bright plumage (feathers), decorative crests and long tails. They display their feathers to females, who choose the most attractive, healthiest looking males to mate with. This helps the females ensure that their chicks will also grow into fine, healthy birds.

A fine-looking male turkey shows off his plumage to attract the females.

OWLS

Owls, such as this Ural owl, are nocturnal birds of prey. They have forward-facing eyes that help them to find their prey of mice and frogs in the night. Some owls hunt fish and other birds.

REPTILES

Reptiles are scaly-skinned vertebrates that lay their eggs on land.

Crocodiles, alligators, turtles, tortoises, snakes and lizards are all types of reptile. Unlike mammals, reptiles cannot make their own body heat, and they have to bask in the sun to get warm. When their bodies are warm, reptiles are able to move faster in search of prey, and digest their food more quickly. At night, reptiles often rest in burrows to avoid losing too much body heat.

REPTILE FEATURES

A crocodile can swim at up to 25 mph (40 km/h) using just its powerful tail. It can stay underwater for 2–3 hours.

Most reptiles lay eggs. Each egg has a tough, leathery coating that protects it, so reptiles can lay their eggs on land. Female reptiles do not usually look after their eggs.

The body of a reptile is covered with thick, horny scales that are made of keratin. These scales protect reptiles from attack, but they also stop the animal's body from drying out in the heat.

Alligators (top) have shorter and broader snouts than crocodiles (bottom). Gharials (opposite page) have extremely slender, long snouts.

GREEN TURTLE

Green turtles live in the oceans and lay their eggs on beaches. They can travel up to 620 miles (1,000 km) to reach the beach they were born on. Young green turtles feed on jellyfish, shelled animals and sponges, but adults eat sea grasses.

CROCODILES AND ALLIGATORS

Crocodiles and alligators mostly live in the rivers and lakes of warm countries. These predators spend most of their time in water, hidden beneath the surface with just their nostrils and eyes visible above it. They lie in wait for prey, such as mammals, to come and drink at the water's edge. They attack with lightning speed and close their powerful jaws around the victim, pulling it below the water.

Crocodiles have hardly changed in 65 million years, when dinosaurs still roamed the Earth. Like other reptiles, they can bite, but not chew.

GHARIALS

Gharials are a type of crocodile that live in Indian rivers. They grab fish in their long jaws and spin them round, so they can swallow them head-first. Gharials are one of the world's most endangered animals.

Gharials are very rare and live only in a small number of places in northern India. Their narrow jaws are lined with rows of sharp teeth. They feed on fish and water birds.

SPOTTER'S GUIDE LIZARDS

Lizards are one of the most successful groups of reptiles, and they live in many different habitats.

Chameleons change their skin tone to attract mates, or if the temperature or light conditions change. They flick out their long, sticky tongues to catch insects.

The frilled lizard has a large frill around its neck that it usually keeps folded, but raises to scare predators.

Thorny devils need a spiny skin to protect them from predators while they feed. These lizards eat ants, which they catch with their tongues.

SNAKES AND LIZARDS

Snakes and lizards are close cousins in the reptile family.

Snakes do not have limbs. They have strong, muscular bodies that move by slithering along the ground, or through trees. Constrictor snakes use their powerful muscles in another way, too. They kill their prey by coiling their bodies around a victim and slowly squeezing it until it can no longer breathe.

DID YOU KNOW?

When attacked, many lizards confuse the enemy by shedding their tails. Then they run for their lives!

This rattlesnake is coiled for attack, ready to lunge forwards, its fangs dripping with deadly venom. Rattlesnakes use their venom to kill prey and for defence.

DEADLY VENOM

Many snakes kill their prey using venom, which is delivered by fangs at the front, or back, of their mouths. They find their prey using keen eyesight, by sensing vibrations through the ground and by "tasting" smells with their tongues. Pit vipers have heat-sensitive pits between their nostrils that can detect the warm body of an animal nearby.

DRAGONS

Komodo dragons can grow to 3 m (10 ft) long and they are the world's heaviest lizards. They live in Indonesia. The dragons use venom in their saliva to help kill their prey. Young Komodo dragons stay in trees to avoid the adults, which might eat them!

DID YOU KNOW?
The inland taipan is the world's most venomous snake. Its venom can kill a human, but it causes very few deaths because it stays away from people.

Boa constrictors grow to 4 m (13 ft) long and are good climbers. They do not lay eggs, but give birth to live young.

IGUANAS

Iguanas, and their relatives, are fast on their feet. They scuttle around looking for food, such as insects, to eat. Like many lizards, iguanas also rely on camouflage to hide – the shades and patterns of their skin help them to "disappear" against their background.

Marine iguanas are able to dive into the sea and stay underwater for up to an hour looking for their seaweed food. Their bodies are adapted to cope with extreme cold and the large amount of salt they encounter.

AMPHIBIANS

Amphibians begin their lives in water, but when they are adult they can live on land.

There are three stages in an amphibian's life cycle: egg, larva and adult. Frogs lay their eggs, or spawn, in ponds. When the eggs hatch, tadpoles (the larvae) emerge. The young live, feed and grow in the water and gradually change into adults. This change is called metamorphosis.

AMPHIBIAN FEATURES

Almost all amphibians have smooth skin, lay eggs in water, and have larvae that look different from the adults.

Amphibian skin is usually thin. Water and gases can move through the skin, so it is often coated with mucus to prevent it from drying out.

Most amphibians abandon their eggs, but this male midwife toad keeps the eggs on his back until they are ready to hatch, then he puts them in water.

Amphibian larvae have gills, which they use to take oxygen from water. This crested newt has long, feathery gills.

DID YOU KNOW?

When newt larvae have finished metamorphosis they are called efts. It may be several years before efts are ready to breed.

A NEW LIFE

Frogs, toads, newts and salamanders are amphibians. They all begin their lives in water, and return to it to breed. However, as adults they can survive on land. Most amphibians prefer to live in damp habitats, hiding under stones or plants.

Common frogs spend most of their adult lives on land, but return to water in spring to mate.

As the tadpoles grow limbs, their tails begin to shorten. They now resemble small frogs.

Newly-hatched tadpoles eat small, green water plants, and quickly develop into mature tadpoles such as these. They grow fastest in warm water.

Male and female frogs mate in water. Females produce clumps of jelly-like frogspawn that swells and floats.

When a green frog jumps, it has to quickly rotate its hind leg joints and bring its legs forwards fast enough for a soft landing, or it will belly-flop!

LEAPS AND HOPS

Frogs and toads are soft-skinned animals, without teeth or claws to defend themselves. One way to escape predators is to jump – and these amphibians, especially frogs, are good jumpers. Their long, muscular legs can launch them into the air, or propel them through water.

Frogs (left) and toads (right) belong to the same group of animals, called anurans. Toads usually have warty skin, spend more time on land than frogs and are walkers rather than leapers. Frogs are smooth-skinned.

FIRE SALAMANDER

The fire salamander has large orange, yellow or red spots on its skin. The spots warn other animals not to try to eat the salamander, because it produces foul-tasting mucus in glands behind its eyes.

FISH FEATURES

Fish scales are made of bone and they overlap one another. They may be different shapes and sizes. Some fish have shiny scales that reflect light to confuse their predators.

A fish's gills are inside its head behind the gill openings (the flaps behind its eyes). Water goes into the fish's mouth and flows through its gills. Oxygen in the water passes into tiny blood vessels, called capillaries, that fill the gills. The water passes out of the gill slits, carrying with it a waste gas, called carbon dioxide.

FISH

Fish have been in the seas for about 500 million years. They breathe using special organs called gills.

Most fish have bodies that are suited for swimming, and are covered in scales. Fish are broadly put into two groups: bony fish and cartilaginous fish. Bony fish have skeletons made of bones. Cartilaginous fish, such as sharks, skates and rays, have skeletons made of a more rubbery material called cartilage.

DID YOU KNOW?
Some male fish protect their eggs by keeping them inside their mouths while they develop.

PIRANHAS

Red piranhas are freshwater fish that are famed for their sharp teeth. According to stories, a shoal of piranhas can attack a horse and shred its body in minutes. In fact, red piranhas do not hunt as shoals, but just take bites from the bodies of passing fish, or feast on animals that are already dead.

BUILT FOR SPEED

Although there are many exceptions, most fish have long, slender bodies that are streamlined. This means they can move through water easily. Their tails are packed with muscles, and fins help fish to change direction and stay upright as they swim.

A school of shimmering mackerel darts through the sea. Their shiny scales reflect light, dazzling larger, hungry fish.

Despite their strange shape, seahorses are bony fish. Males look after the eggs in a special pouch, and give birth to the fry.

DID YOU KNOW?

Deep sea anglerfish live far down in the ocean. To attract prey, they have a long spine above their mouth that ends in a piece of flesh that glows in the dark.

All seahorses are poor swimmers. They have to wind their tails around seaweed to prevent themselves from being carried away by ocean currents.

FRY TO FISH

After mating, female fish lay their eggs. Sometimes, the parents guard the eggs from predators. After growing, the eggs hatch and baby fish, called fry, emerge. They are vulnerable to attack from other animals, so fry often hide in seaweed, or in holes in rocks, to avoid being eaten. Most females lay lots of eggs, because few fry survive to adulthood.

SHARKS, SKATES AND RAYS

SPOTTER'S GUIDE SHARKS

The smallest sharks are just 16–19 cm (6–7 in) long. Whale sharks are 50 times longer.

The massive basking shark swims with its mouth open, swallowing plankton.

Zebra sharks feed on crabs, mollusks and shrimps.

Whale sharks are the largest fish in the world.

Nurse sharks suck their prey off the seafloor.

The first cartilaginous fish evolved in the seas about 370 million years ago.

Cartilaginous fish are different from bony fish in three main ways. Their skeletons are made of cartilage, which bends more easily than bone, their skin is covered with teeth-like scales called denticles, and their teeth replace themselves throughout their lives.

SHARKS

Sharks have streamlined bodies and many of them are fast-swimming hunters that pursue prey through the water. Their large, powerful jaws are equipped with rows of sharp teeth and they have an excellent sense of smell that helps them to find prey.

Grey reef sharks were common in coral reefs, but their numbers are falling and research is being done to find out why. They feed on small fish and give birth to young called pups.

DID YOU KNOW?

About one-third of all cartilaginous fish are threatened with extinction. This is due to the loss of their habitats, and the effects of overfishing.

SKATES AND RAYS

Skates and rays have flattened bodies and often spend their lives on the seafloor. Manta rays, however, swim in the open ocean. Their large, broad bodies have fins that work like underwater wings, enabling these huge fish to swim while sucking tiny animals, called plankton, out of the water. Manta rays can grow to 7 m (23 ft) long.

Manta rays live in warm waters and are solitary animals. Despite their fearsome looks, these rays are harmless.

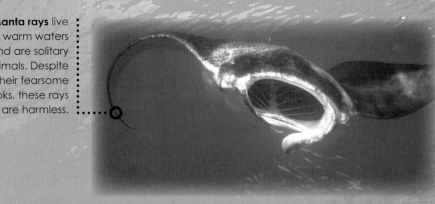

Most sharks have dark backs and pale undersides. This helps the shark to stay hidden when seen both from above and from below.

When a fish moves its muscles, it creates a small electrical current. Tiny holes in a shark's skin enable it to detect this electricity and locate its prey with great accuracy.

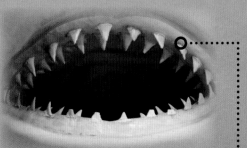

A shark's teeth grow in several rows. Every time a shark catches prey it will lose some teeth, but new ones move forward to replace them.

GREAT WHITE SHARK

The great white shark is widely feared, but these large fish rarely attack humans. They are incredible swimmers and have huge teeth that are perfect for grabbing and ripping at prey, such as seals and other sharks. Unlike most fish, great whites are able to control their body temperature, which helps them achieve great swimming speeds.

INSECT FEATURES

Most insects have compound eyes. Each eye is made up of lots of tiny lenses and each sends a different image to the insect's brain.

Head

Thorax

Abdomen.

An insect's body is divided into three parts: the head, thorax and abdomen. Legs and wings are attached to the thorax. Organs used in reproduction and digesting food are in the abdomen.

Adult insects have three pairs of legs. The legs have joints that enable them to bend. Many insects also have wings.

CREEPY CRAWLIES

Animals that do not have skeletons inside their bodies are called invertebrates.

Insects, crustaceans, worms and spiders are all types of invertebrate. Of these, insects are the most successful. They are able to survive in almost every type of habitat on land. Insects have a tough outer skin, called an exoskeleton. Beetles, flies, ants, moths and grasshoppers are all insects.

Grasshoppers are plant-eating insects that mostly live in grasslands. They can form giant swarms that devour entire crops.

DID YOU KNOW?

More than one million species of insects have been found so far, but there are probably millions more!

An adult cicada crawls out of its old exoskeleton. Young cicadas (nymphs) look like the adults, but lack wings.

INSECT LARVAE AND NYMPHS

Many insects, such as flies, butterflies and beetles, have young, called larvae, that look very different from the adults. When the larvae change into adults, they go through a process called metamorphosis. Other insects have young, called nymphs, that resemble the adults. When an insect grows, it has to shed its old exoskeleton to reveal a new one underneath.

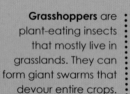

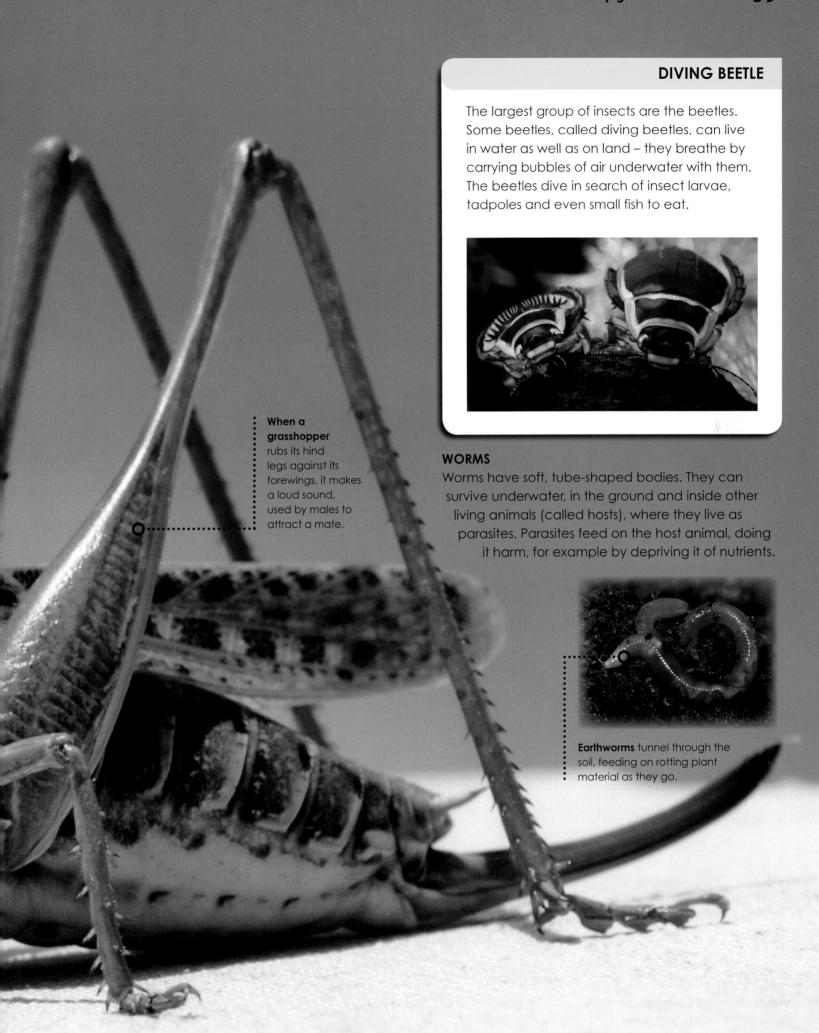

DIVING BEETLE

The largest group of insects are the beetles. Some beetles, called diving beetles, can live in water as well as on land – they breathe by carrying bubbles of air underwater with them. The beetles dive in search of insect larvae, tadpoles and even small fish to eat.

When a grasshopper rubs its hind legs against its forewings, it makes a loud sound, used by males to attract a mate.

WORMS

Worms have soft, tube-shaped bodies. They can survive underwater, in the ground and inside other living animals (called hosts), where they live as parasites. Parasites feed on the host animal, doing it harm, for example by depriving it of nutrients.

Earthworms tunnel through the soil, feeding on rotting plant material as they go.

SPIDER FEATURES

Some spiders grab hold of their prey and sink their chelicerae (fangs) into the prey's body.

Some female spiders use many layers of silk to make an egg sac, which they place on their web.

Few spiders look after their young, but this wolf spider keeps her babies on her back.

Males are often smaller than the females. They may also have different patterns on their bodies.

SPIDERS AND SCORPIONS

Spiders and scorpions are land-living invertebrate. They belong to the same family – arachnids.

Spiders and scorpions have eight legs, bodies that are divided into two parts, and up to eight eyes. They are able to make silk – a super-strong and stretchy material that they use to trap prey. Spiders are predators – they hunt insects and other spiders. Most of them have venom, which they use to paralyse and kill their prey.

SUPER SILK

All spiders are able to make silk in their abdomens. A strand of silk can stretch six times a spider's own length before snapping, and is proportionally stronger than steel. A spider guides the thread as it emerges from its body and uses it to create webs, or traps, or silken cocoons to protect its eggs.

DID YOU KNOW?
Some spiders inject burning juices into their prey's body, which turns to liquid inside. The spider sucks out the liquid, leaving just the tough, empty skin behind.

Wolf spiders are nocturnal predators. They have good eyesight, but recognize their prey by the sound of their beating wings, or by sensing their movements.

Emperor scorpions are large, but their venom is mild. They prey on small animals, such as crickets, termites, mice and beetles.

SCORPIONS

Scorpions are related to spiders and are among the largest of all land-living invertebrates. Their front legs are shaped like claws and their tails bear venomous stings. Females give birth to baby scorpions, which they carry on their backs. Scorpions are most commonly found in warm places. They often hide under stones, or in burrows and usually hunt at night.

JUMPING SPIDER

Jumping spiders do not spin webs to catch their prey – they hunt them instead. They have superb eyesight and a good sense of smell. Once they have located their prey, some jumping spiders can pounce and cover a distance 20 times greater than their body length.

Underwater world

The oceans and seas are home to billions of living things.

Watery habitats cover more than 70 per cent of the world's surface, and most of them are marine – filled with salty, not fresh, water. This environment is where life began, and where more complex animals evolved about 540 million years ago. Today, the underwater world contains a huge range of animals, from ones that are so small they can only be seen with a microscope, to enormous whales, squid and fish.

DID YOU KNOW?

Japanese spider crabs can measure 4 m (13 ft) from the tip of one outstretched leg to the tip of another.

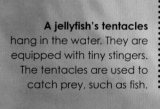

A jellyfish's tentacles hang in the water. They are equipped with tiny stingers. The tentacles are used to catch prey, such as fish.

A topshell is a type of mollusk. The tough shell protects the soft-bodied grazing animal hidden within.

JELLYFISH

There are many soft-bodied animals in the oceans. They can grow large without a skeleton, or an exoskeleton, because the water supports their weight. Jellyfish can grow up to 1 m (3 ft) wide, and they have long, stinging tentacles that hang from the body, or bell.

CRUSTACEANS

Crabs, lobsters and shrimps are crustaceans. They have two pairs of antennae, or sensitive feelers, on their heads, compound eyes on stalks and a tough outer skin called a carapace.

Mantis shrimps wallop their prey with powerful, spear-like limbs.

MOLLUSKS

One of the most varied groups of marine animals is the mollusk group. Octopuses, sea slugs and shelled creatures are all mollusks. These animals are soft-bodied, but many of them have a tough outer skin, or shell, which protects them from predators. While some mollusks seem to be simple animals with small brains, others, such as octopuses, are known to be intelligent – they can find their way through mazes and change color to hide from predators.

SPINY SKIN

Echinoderms are an unusual group of marine animals. Their outer skin is toughened with calcium carbonate, which is similar to the mix of minerals that makes human teeth strong. Most echinoderms have spines. Starfish and sea urchins are types of echinoderms.

Starfish

Sea urchin

DID YOU KNOW?

Octopuses in captivity have worked out how to open screw-top jars, to reach food inside. They can recognize patterns and even use coconut shells to hide in.

A common octopus can grow to 1 m (40 in) long. Good at camouflage, it can change the pattern and shade of its skin to suit its mood or situation.

EXTREME ANIMALS

Scientists are always discovering record-breaking animals. Impress your friends with some extreme animal facts.

Animals are able to live in almost every habitat on Earth because they can change, improve and find new ways to survive. This has led to the development of some weird and wonderful animals.

The male proboscis monkey has an enormous nose. Sometimes when it is running, its nose can flip back and hit it in the eye!

A golden eagle can see a rabbit moving more than 1.25 miles (2 km) away, and a peregrine falcon can spy a pigeon flying 5 miles (8 km) away.

Bootlace worms can grow to be 55 m (181 ft) long.

The largest earthworms in the world are as thick as your arm.

Whales talk to each other, and make the loudest sounds of any animal. A whale bellow can be as loud as a rocket taking off.

Sailfish can slice through the water at top speeds of 68 mph (109 km/h). This makes them faster than a cheetah. They need to swim fast to be able to chase schools of smaller fish, such as anchovies and sardines.

Spotted skunks are the smelliest animals around. They produce a foul stink to scare away other animals.

TOXIC TERRORS

Gaboon vipers (above) have long fangs that can pump venom far into their victims' muscles. One bite has enough venom to kill ten people!

Golden poison-dart frogs have toxic skin. The chemicals are so deadly that one touch of their soft, wet skin can kill.

Sea wasps are jellyfish with long, dangling tentacles that are covered with stingers. The stings cause terrible pain, and sometimes even death.

ANIMALS IN TROUBLE

An animal is said to be endangered when it is at risk of becoming extinct. How many of these animals will still be around in 100 years?

The African lion once roamed over most of Africa, but it is now endangered in many areas. One third of all lions have been killed in the last 20 years.

Southern bluefin tuna are fished by humans for food. Their population has fallen by 80 per cent in recent years, and they are close to being totally wiped out.

The Javan rhino is the rarest of the five types of rhinoceros. There are only about 50 individuals left.

The kakapo is a large, flightless parrot. Kakapos are being looked after carefully, and their numbers have doubled in the last ten years from about 60 to 120.

The giant panda is used as the symbol for endangered animals everywhere. Only about 1,600 giant pandas survive in the wild at present.

Giant tortoises live on islands in the Indian and Pacific oceans. They can weigh as much as three adult men. They are also one of the longest-living animals on the planet. One giant tortoise died at the age of 175.

Giraffes are huge, but it is not just their bodies that are big. They have extra-long tongues that measure 50 cm (20 in) in length!

GLOSSARY

Bamboo Tall-growing grass that grows mainly in warm places.

Canid A member of the dog family, such as wolves and jackals.

Carnivore An animal whose diet is mostly, or entirely, made up of meat.

Cartilaginous Having a skeleton made of a material called cartilage, which bends more easily than bone.

Climate A region's long-term weather patterns, such as temperature, rainfall and wind.

Crest Many birds have decorative feathers on their heads that are known as crests. These may be used to impress mates.

Crustacean Animals with four or more pairs of limbs, bodies that are divided into segments and tough exoskeletons. Most crustaceans live in aquatic habitats.

Echolocation A way of finding things that uses the echoes that are created by sound bouncing off objects and surfaces. Bats and dolphins hunt using echolocation.

Environment The place and surroundings where a living thing survives and that affect its growth.

Equator An imaginary line that circles the Earth at an equal distance from the North and South Poles.

Evolution The process by which living things change and adapt over many generations to suit the conditions of the environment.

Extinct When all members of a species of animal or plant have died out, the species is said to be extinct.

Freshwater Water that has only low levels of salts in it, such as rain, river, pond and lake water.

Fry Baby fish

Gill An organ used to take oxygen out of water, and to pass the waste gas (carbon dioxide) out of the body.

Grassland A large area of country that is covered with grass. Also known as savannah, prairie or steppe.

Habitat The place where a living thing exists. The term can include all the other living things in that space, and the climate.

Herbivore An animal whose diet is mostly, or entirely, made up of plants.

Invertebrate An animal that does not have a backbone. Mollusks, worms and insects are invertebrates.

Keratin Nails, feathers, hair, scales and hooves are made of keratin.

Larva A young insect or amphibian. More than one are larvae.

Life cycle The story of a plant or animal's life, including reproduction (having young), ageing and death.

Limb Arms, legs and wings are all types of limb.

Mammal A vertebrate animal that has hair or fur, gives birth and produces milk for its young.

Marsupial A type of mammal that gives birth to very small and undeveloped young, which are looked after in a pouch on the mother's body.

Migration A long journey, often undertaken to reach water, food or mating areas.

Monotreme A type of unusual mammal that lays eggs.

Nectar A sweet, sugary liquid produced by flowers.

Nocturnal Active at night.

Nymph The younger stage of some insects. Nymphs resemble the adults, but their wings have not developed.

Pollution Substances that enter an environment, and harm it, are said to be causing pollution and are described as pollutants.

Predator An animal that hunts and attacks other animals for food.

Prey An animal that is hunted by predators and eaten.

Primate A type of mammal with a large brain that shows complex ways of living. Primates are able to pinch with a finger and thumb.

Species A type of animal or plant that can only mate with others of the same type.

Termite A small, pale, ant-like insect that lives in large colonies.

Venom A poison made by animals and usually inserted into another animal with a sting or bite.

Vertebrate An animal with a backbone.

INDEX

CREDITS
Text written by: Camilla de la Bedoyere

PICTURES
D = Dreamstime.com, Sh = Shutterstock.com, Th = Thinkstock.com.
t = top, b = bottom, l = left, r = right, c = centre.

Page 1 Sh/ © Kwan Fah Mun. Pages 2-3 top row (left to right 1-16) 1. Sh/ © Indric, 2. Sh/ © hainaultphoto, 3. Sh/ © Dennis Donohue, 4. Th/ © Getty Images/Jupiterimages, 5. Sh/ © mlorenz, 6. Th/ iStockphoto, 7. Sh/ © Ronald van der Beek, 8. Sh/ © TOMO, 9. Sh/ © Krzysztof Odziomek, 10. Sh/ © dean bertoncelj, 11. Sh/ © kwest, 12. Sh/ © BogdanBoev, 13. Sh/ © alarifoto, 14. Sh/ © Rich Carey, 15. © Sh/ Eduard Kyslynskyy, 16. Sh/ © Elisei Shafer. Pages 2-3 bl Sh/ © Eric Isselée, 2-3 br Sh/ © Vlad61, 4tl Sh/ © Indric, 4cl Th/ iStockphoto, 4bl Th/ iStockphoto, 4r Sh/ © Benis Arapovic, 5tl Sh/ © Matthew Cole, 5cl Sh/ © RembeX, 5tr (anticlockwise 1-7) 1. Sh/ © Eric Isselée, 2. Sh/ © holbox, 3. Sh/ © Neo Edmund, 4. Sh/ © Eric Isselée,

5. Sh/ © Audrey Snider-Bell, 6. Sh/ © Eric Isselée, 7. Sh/ © Stephen Mcsweeny, 5cr Sh/ © Knorre, 5br Sh/ © Indric, 6l (top to bottom 1-4) 1. Sh/ © Vlad61, 2. Sh/ © Vitaly Titov & Maria Sidelnikova, 3. Sh/ © hainaultphoto, 4. Sh/ © Algol, 6b Sh/ © Sam Chadwick, 7tr Sh/ © Sergey Karpov, 7 (main) Sh/ © Vlad61, 8l (top to bottom 1-4) 1. Sh/ © Smileus, 2. Sh/ © Sergey Mat, 3. Sh/ © Nagel Photography, 4. Sh/ © Dennis Donohue, 8br D/ © Robgubiani, 9tr © Peter Scheunis, 9 (main) Sh/ © Smileus, 8-9 (background) Sh/ © iofoto, 10tl Sh/ © mlorenz, 10tr Th/ © Getty Images/ Jupiterimages, 10b Sh/ © Mogens Trolle, 11tl Norbert Sipos/Beehive Art Agency, 11 (main) Sh/ © Ecoimages, 12bl Sh/ © Mike Flippo, 12tr Th/ © Tom Brakefield, 13 (main) Sh/ © Alaskan Guide, 13 br © AEPhotographic, 14bl Th/ iStockphoto, 14tr Sh/ © Geoffrey Kuchera, 14-15 (main) Sh/ © Eric Isselée, 15tr Sh/ © Gail Johnson, 15cr Sh/ © YorkBerlin, 16tl Th/ Hemera, 16cl Sh/ © Ronald van der Beek, 16b Sh/ © Uryadnikov Sergey, 16tr Th/ © Tom Brakefield, 17bl Sh/ © Sharon Day, 17tl Sh/ © worldswildlifewonders, 17r Th/ Hemera, 18tr Norbert Sipos/Beehive Art Agency, 18cl Sh/ © argonaut, 18bl Sh/ © Adam Brokeš, 18br Sh/ © Eric Isselée, 19cl Sh/ © javarman, 19 (main) Sh/ © EcoPrint, 20l (top to bottom 1-5) 1. Sh/ © TOMO, 2. Sh/ © Andrea Danti, 3. Sh/ © Andrea Danti, 4. Sh/ © Andrea Danti, 5. Sh/ © Karina Wallton, 20-21 (main) Sh/ © idreamphoto, 21tr Sh/ © Krzysztof Odziomek, 21c Sh/ © TOMO, 22l (top to bottom 1-4) 1. Sh/ © alarifoto, 2. Sh/ © Faded Beauty, 3. Sh/ © dean bertoncelj, 4. Sh/ © Filip Fuxa, 22-23 (main) Sh/ © Johan Swanepoel, 23tr Sh/ © Marty Ellis, 23c Sh/ © alarifoto, 23bl Sh/ © MartinMaritz, 23br Sh/ © liubomir, 24bl Sh/ © kwest, 24-25 (main foreground) Sh/ © wim claes, 24-25 (background) Sh/ © Anna Omelchenko, 25tr Sh/ © Glenn Price, 25br Sh/ © BogdanBoev, 26bl Sh/ © Michael G. Mill, 26-27 (main) Sh/ © dirkr, 27bl Sh/ © Bruce MacQueen, 27br Sh/ © alarifoto, 28l (top to bottom 1-4) 1. Sh/ © Labetskiy Alexandr Alexandrovich, 2. Sh/ © Netfalls, 3. Sh/ © Trevor kelly, 4. Sh/ © iofoto, 28tr (top to bottom 1-2) 1. Sh/ © Eric Isselée, 2. Sh/ © seaskylab, 28c Sh/ © Rich Carey, 28-29 (main) Sh/ © Labetskiy Alexandr Alexandrovich, 29tr Sh/ © Dirtfoto, 30l (top to bottom 1-4) 1. Sh/ © cellistka, 2. Sh/ © Eduard Kyslynskyy, 3. Sh/ © kkaplin, 4. Sh/ © Janelle Lugge, 30tr Sh/ © Maria Dryfhout, 30br Sh/ © Uryadnikov Sergey, 31 (main) Sh/ © cellistka, 31bl Sh/ © Uryadnikov Sergey, 32l (top to bottom 1-4) 1. Sh/ © photobank.kiev.ua, 2. Sh/ © Steven Russell Smith Photos, 3. Norbert Sipos/Beehive Art Agency, 4. Sh/ © Dirk Ercken, 32-33 (main) Sh/ © Mircea BEZERGHEANU, 33tr Th/ © John Foxx, 33cr (left) Sh/ © imagestalk, 33cr (right) Sh/ © Jens61er, 33cl (top to bottom 1-3) 1. Sh/ Dr. Morley Read, 2. Sh/ © Wolfgang Staib, 3. Sh/ Birute Vijeikiene, 33br Sh/ © photobank.kiev.ua, 34l (top to bottom 1-4) 1. Sh/ © melissaf84, 2. Sh/ © Eric Isselée, 3. Sh/ © schankz, 4. Sh/ © Stefanie Mohr Photography, 34tr Sh/ © guentermanaus, 34br Sh/ © goldenangel, 35 Sh/ © melissaf84, 36l (top to bottom 1-5) 1. Sh/ © Darryl Brooks, 2. © Greg Skomal/SWFSC-NOAA, 3. Sh/ © Christophe Rouziou, 4. Sh/ © Krzysztof Odziomek, 5. Sh/ © Lawrence Cruciana, 36-37 (main) Sh/ © Rich Carey, 37tr Sh/ © Circumnavigation, 37bl (top) Sh/ © stockpix4u, 37bl (bottom) Sh/ © Darryl Brooks, 37br Sh/ © Roger De Marfa, 38l (top to bottom 1-4) 1. Sh/ © Dirk Ercken, 2. Sh/ © StudioNewmarket, 3. Sh/ © R-photos, 4. Sh/ © Papik, 38tr Sh/ © vblinov, 38-39 (main) Sh/ © Gala_Kan, 39tr Sh/ © Dirk Ercken, 39br Sh/ © Vinicius Tupinamba, 40l (top to bottom 1-5) 1. Sh/ © Cathy Keifer, 2. Sh/ © Cathy Keifer, 3. Sh/ © Cathy Keifer, 4. Sh/ © orionmystery@flickr, 5. Sh/ © Pan Xunbin, 40br Sh/ © Audrey Snider-Bell, 41 (main) Sh/ © Cathy Keifer, 41br Sh/ © Cathy Keifer, 42bl Sh/ © ECOSTOCK, 42-43 (main) Sh/ © vilainecrevette, 43tl Sh/ © Image Focus, 43tr (top) Sh/ © Elisei Shafer, 43tr (bottom) Sh/ © almondd, 43bl Sh/ © Vittorio Bruno, 44bl Sh/ © Webitect, 44tr Sh/ © Catmando, 44br Sh/ © Andreas Meyer, 45tl Sh/ © EcoPrint, 45tr Sh/ © M Reel, 45br Sh/ © markrhiggins.

Poster: All poster images are taken from the book, as credited above.